LIFE IN EARLY CANADA

FOOD

Alexis Roumanis

Weigl

Published by Weigl Educational Publishers Limited
6325 10th Street SE
Calgary, Alberta T2H 2Z9

Website: www.weigl.ca

Copyright ©2013 Weigl Educational Publishers Limited

Library and Archives Canada Cataloguing in Publication data available upon request.
Fax 403-233-7769 for the attention of the Publishing Records department.

ISBN 978-1-77071-221-8 (hard cover)
ISBN 978-1-77071-235-5 (soft cover)

Printed in the United States of America in North Mankato, Minnesota
1 2 3 4 5 6 7 8 9 0 16 15 14 13 12

072012
WEP250612

Project Coordinator: Alexis Roumanis
Design: Mandy Christiansen

Weigl acknowledges Getty Images as the primary image supplier for this title.

We acknowledge the financial support of the Government of Canada through the Canada Book Fund for our publishing activities.

LIFE IN EARLY CANADA

FOOD

CONTENTS

4 Introduction

6 Inuit

8 Tsuu T'ina

10 Mi'kmaq

12 Assiniboine

14 English

16 Scottish

18 Dutch

20 Greek

22 Life in Early Canada Facts

24 Activity

In Canada's early years, different peoples learned from each other.

Aboriginal Peoples taught settlers how to find food. Settlers traded metal pots to Aboriginal Peoples in return.

The Inuit lived in Canada's Far North.

They hunted narwhal for food.

The Tsuu T'ina were from the south part of Alberta.

They rode on horses to hunt bison.

The Mi'kmaq lived in Atlantic Canada and Quebec.

They caught salmon from rivers and the Atlantic Ocean.

The Assiniboine lived in Saskatchewan.

They hunted elk to feed their families.

Many English people came to Canada to become fur trappers.

They hunted mountain goats in the Canadian Rockies.

Scottish people came to Canada to own land.

Many Scottish people grew wheat in Atlantic Canada.

The Dutch came to Canada to grow food on farms.

They grew corn on
the Canadian prairies.

Many Greek people came to Canada to start businesses.

Some Greeks planted fig trees when they came to Canada.

LIFE IN EARLY CANADA FACTS

These pages provide detailed information that expands on the interesting facts found in the book. These pages are intended to be used by adults as a learning support to help young readers round out their knowledge of each group of people featured in *Life in Early Canada*.

Pages 4–5

Canada became a country in 1867. First Nations, Inuit, Métis, and immigrants from all over the world helped form Canada. Life in early Canada was difficult for many settlers, but they received help from indigenous peoples. These peoples taught settlers how to hunt, fish, plant crops, build canoes, and stay warm during cold Canadian winters.

Pages 6–7

The Inuit are from Canada. They inhabit the northern regions of Canada, from the Pacific to the Atlantic Oceans. Many Inuit lived in igloos and travelled across vast expanses of snow and ice using dogsleds. The Inuit in what is now the territory of Nunavut hunted narwhals for their skin, which was eaten raw with a layer of fat. The Inuit called this food *Muktaaq*. They also used the narwhal tusk to make knives.

Pages 8–9

The Tsuu T'ina are from Canada. Though they were originally from northern Canada, the Tsuu T'ina eventually settled on the plains of southern Alberta. The Tsuu T'ina lived closely with other First Nations in Alberta. They hunted, camped, and travelled together. The Tsuu T'ina followed bison herds, moving their villages as the bison travelled.

Pages 10–11

The Mi'kmaq are from Canada. They are indigenous to Atlantic Canada and Quebec. The Mi'kmaq were semi-nomadic, moving to where food was plentiful at different times of the year. They hunted animals such as caribou, moose, and deer. They also fished for lobster, eel, and salmon.

Pages 12–13

The Assiniboine are from Canada. They lived on the plains of Saskatchewan. The Assiniboine were excellent hunters. They used the bow and arrow to hunt. The Assiniboine were semi-nomadic, moving with the migration patterns of bison herds. Any bison meat they did not eat during summer was preserved and stored for winter.

Pages 14–15

The English are from Europe. Many English people came to Canada to own farmland. English settlements were established by the Hudson's Bay Company to gather fur. One such settlement was built at what is now known as Jasper National Park. Mountain goats were plentiful in the area. These animals are excellent mountain climbers. The English hunted mountain goats for food.

Pages 16–17

The Scottish are from Europe. In the early 18th century, Scottish Highlanders settled on the Atlantic coast of Canada. They left Scotland to pursue political and religious freedom. Many Scottish farmers came to Canada because they lost their farmland at home. Scottish farmers grew wheat, hemp, and apples. Today, Canadians of Scottish descent are the third largest ethnic group in Canada.

Pages 18–19

The Dutch are from Europe. Dutch people came to Canada in large numbers toward the end of the 19th century. They left the Netherlands because there were not enough jobs for all of the agricultural workers in the country. The Dutch primarily settled in the Canadian prairies. Many Dutch settlers grew wheat, corn, and barley.

Pages 20–21

Greeks are from Europe. They came to Canada at the turn of the 19th century. Many Greeks were refugees from what is now known as Turkey, where they were forced to leave their lands. Greeks mostly settled in Montreal and Toronto. They became entrepreneurs in restaurants, delis, coffee shops, and other businesses. Many Greeks brought seeds from their homeland, such as figs, grapes, and artichokes.

ACTIVITY

Match the people with their food.

Scottish   English   Mi'kmaq   Assiniboine
Dutch   Greek   Tsuu T'ina   Inuit

1. Mi'kmaq 2. Dutch 3. Inuit 4. Scottish 5. Greek 6. Assiniboine 7. Tsuu T'ina 8. English

24